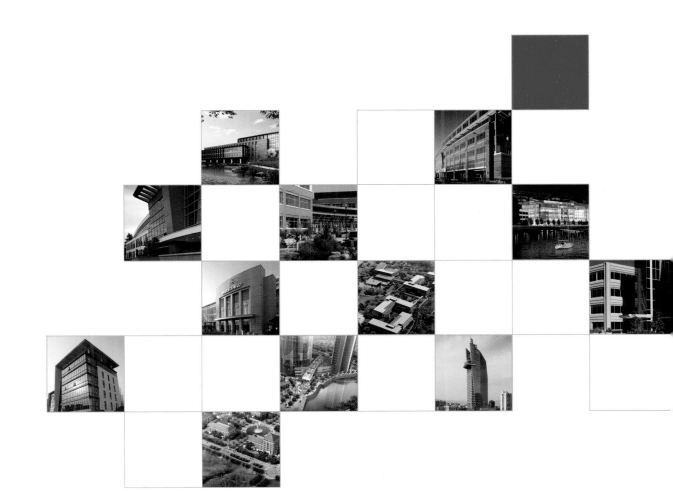

DESIGN AT WORK

Copyright © 2008 by Visual Reference Publications, Inc.

Library of Congress Cataloging in Publication Data: Corporate Interiors No. 8

ISBN: 978-1-58471-110-0   ISBN: 1-58471-110-8

Distributors to the trade in the United States and Canada
Watson-Guptill
770 Broadway
New York, NY 10003

Distributors outside the United States and Canada
HarperCollins International
10 East 53rd Street
New York, NY 10022-5299

Printed and bound in China

DESIGN AT WORK

A Different Kind of Success Story

All architects are created equal, like the rest of humanity, without being created alike. Some are gifted designers. Others are expert technicians. There are even those who are formidable managers.

Occasionally, someone appears who does more than one thing well. Consider MulvannyG2 Architecture, a Bellevue, Washington-based firm with a global presence. MulvannyG2 possesses core competencies in the design of retail, residential high-rise, mixed-use, hospitality and office buildings, and provides services in architecture, planning and interior design.

Though not characterized as a "celebrity architect," MulvannyG2 is America's sixteenth largest architecture firm (Building Design & Construction, 2007), fourth largest retail design firm (Visual Merchandising + Store Design, 2007), and one of the fastest growing firms overall. Starting with a studio founded by Doug Mulvanny in 1971, it now fields a workforce of some 500 employees located in Portland, Oregon, Irvine, California, Washington, DC, and Shanghai, China, as well as the headquarters in Bellevue—a short drive from Seattle. The range of projects from MulvannyG2 includes everything from modest interiors to entire campuses.

How has MulvannyG2 become a formidable shaper of spaces, buildings and communities? The firm cites a number of factors. It has an effective business model that combines client service, process management and technical design excellence. It has market and design expertise in its core markets. (To the delight of clients, it defines "design" broadly enough to enlist everyone who touches a project, including the bean counters tracking costs, in making improvements.) It has a company culture that celebrates cultural diversity among employees and clients worldwide. It has a corporate philosophy that values giving back to the community by supporting employee participation in a variety of non-profit organizations.

These factors are telling in many ways. Take the firm's retail rollouts for most of Costco's 500-plus stores. To survive in work like this, you have to be methodical, efficient and reliable- and very, very fast. Look at its projects for such corporations and institutions as Boeing, Hyatt, Fujian Provincial Electric and Power Company, OPUS, Hines, Northwest and the City of Tacoma, Washington. Such clients expect an architect to be customer-focused, value-minded and adaptable. Are these values prized by today's clients? Absolutely.

Yet MulvannyG2 can also give clients more than solid projects delivered on time and budget. Forget for a moment that its design for the new City Hall in Redmond, Washington was chosen over submissions by more famous competitors, and take a good long look at the result. Here's an exciting, innovative and thoughtfully designed example of modern architecture with an inspiring "public living room" at its heart. With work like this, MulvannyG2 will surely convince clients that good design is good business in the United States and around the world.

Roger Yee
Editorial Director, Visual Reference Publications

Counted among the most famous international architectural design firms, MulvannyG2 Architecture's exceptional success has built a reputation for high-quality architectural design.

MulvannyG2 was established in 1971 and has formed a comprehensive international team throughout the world, having designed and completed projects in all 50 of the United States, Canada, Mexico, Asia, China, Australia and the Middle East, including over 40 projects in the Chinese cities of Beijing, Tianjin, Shanghai, Suzhou, Nanjing, Fuzhou and Xiamen. The company uses its far reaching vision, the latest concepts and outstanding service to expand its footprint in the design market with a range of services, from planning, to construction and interior design. With 37 years of experience and a global team, the company has used its base near Seattle to expand throughout the U.S. and into the international arena; building its brand on the concepts of "originality" and "design at work," showing exceptional talent in design planning for retailers, high-tech parks, headquarters of multinationals, and high-end hotels, receiving a number of awards and recognitions.

I have been lucky enough to interview, visit and view MulvannyG2, personally experiencing the soul of this company, which is focused on innovation and effective management, as well as its sense of teamwork and cultural cohesion. The company has employees from all backgrounds and cultures, providing a global information platform in 19 languages. The company's management is sensitive, trustworthy and united. Senior Partners Ming Zhang and Mitch Smith are expansion-minded individuals, who are putting their all into world-class projects. I listened in on design discussions, which clearly focused on a design concept with an emphasis on the global environment, green construction, putting people first and respect for the customer. After attending a great company-wide breakfast meeting, I really felt the vitality of its corporate culture, promoting passion, and fostering knowledge and exploration. This has become the basis for MulvannyG2's creation of outstanding architecture. Standing in front of completed structures designed by MulvannyG2, I truly felt their harmony with the environment, their return to nature, their innovation, concept of green construction and the infectious nature of their architectural artistry.

MulvannyG2 has expanded internationally. From the U.S. to China, the company's fame and recognition have become broader and deeper, becoming the architectural firm of choice for many world industry leaders and a company that can be trusted. I hope that MulvannyG2 will continue its successful run.

Xing Tonghe, Chief Architect (Senior)
Shanghai Xian Dai Architectural Design (Group) Co., Ltd.

Great design begins
with passion.

Ming Zhang, AIA
Senior Partner, Design Director

How has a design firm headquartered in the Northwestern United States been so successful in creating outstanding spaces around the world? The answer lies in one word: relevance. Whatever the project, wherever it is located, we are dogged in our pursuit of innovative design that is unwaveringly relevant to whatever result you want to achieve.

At the heart of our work lies energetic collaboration and spirited dialogue. First, we listen. We internalize your needs and aspirations so that, together, we can clearly define your project's objectives—your intention. Then we will invite you to be open to new possibilities, and we will surprise and delight you with solutions you might not expect.

Such work is only possible because of our exceptional people—globally savvy, culturally astute, and remarkably talented professionals who unfailingly deliver innovative ideas and a seamless customer experience. From our architects to our project managers to our accounting staff, design—the art of making a space more compelling to users, more beautiful, more sustainable, and more profitable—is part of everyone's job description.

Excellent design has little to do with longitude and latitude. Rather, it is the inevitable result when design harmonizes with intention. Every day, our design works for thousands of people living, doing business, and playing in communities around the world. We'd like to show you how our design can work for you. Thank you for your interest in MulvannyG2 Architecture.

Sincerely,

Ming Zhang, AIA
Senior Partner, Design Director
MulvannyG2 Architecture

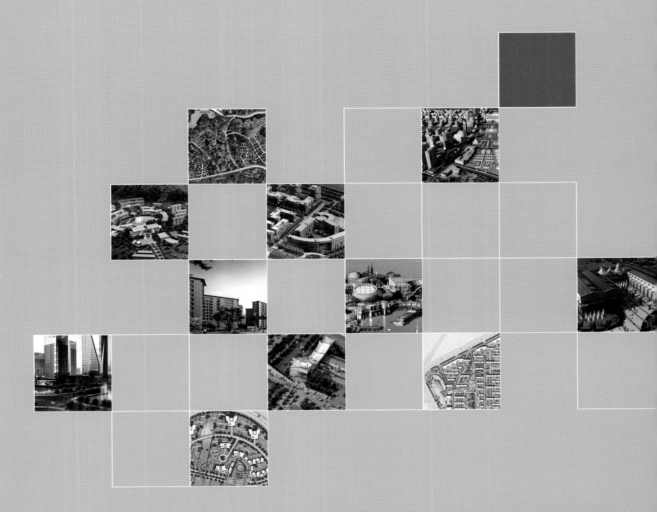

Master Planning | Urban Design

Minhang Business Center
MINGHANG, CHINA

Shanghai, Minhang District Government

188 Acres

Dalian Outsourcing Center

DALIAN, CHINA

Dalian Yida Group

3,200 Acres

The Landing at Evergreen
VANCOUVER, WASHINGTON

OPUS Northwest

50 Acres

Qingdao Techological University
QINGDAO, CHINA

Qingdao Technological University

161 Acres

Sun City Arabia
MANAMA, BAHRAIN

Apex Investment Group

576 Acres

Jinan East New City Master Plan

JINAN, CHINA

Jinan Building and Planning Department

8 Square Miles

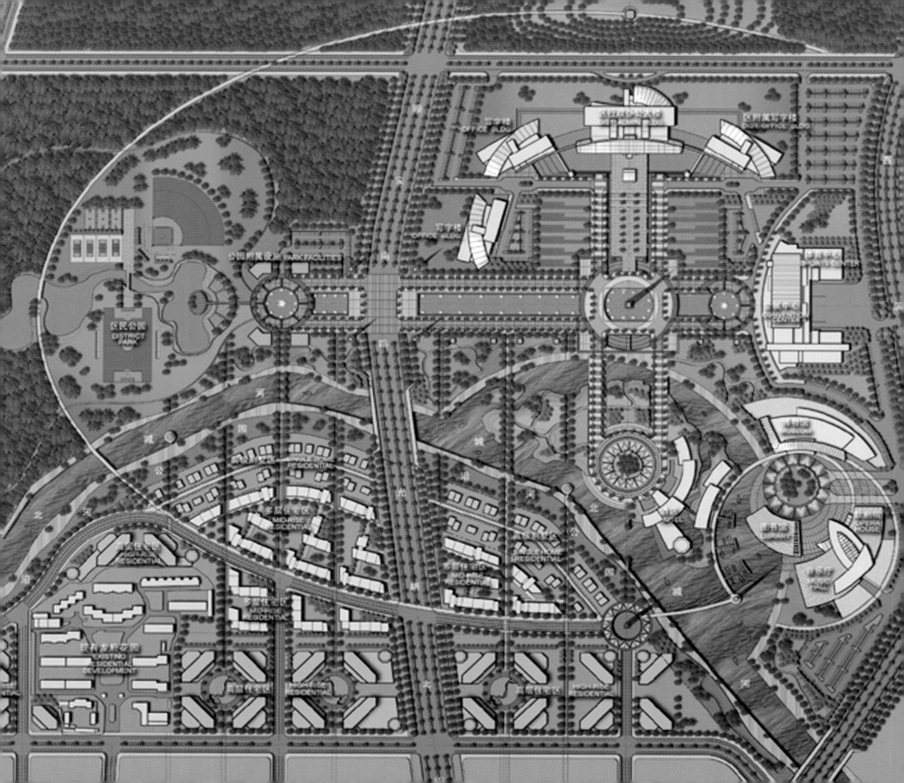

Beijing Shunyi District Olympic Land Use Planning and Administration Center

BEIJING, CHINA

Beijing Shunyi District Government

16 Square Miles (Planning Area)

358 Acres (Administration Center)

"Urban Green Valley" Shenyang Behai New Residential District

SHENYANG, CHINA

Shenyang Wanheng Hongji Real

Estate Development Co. Ltd.

142 Acres

Hangzhou Mingdu
Residential Planning
HANGZHOU, CHINA

Wenzhou Mingdu Real Estate

Development Co., Ltd.

600,000 Square Feet

Shanghai Expo 2010
SHANGHAI, CHINA

Area TBD

Corporate Office

Boeing World Headquarters

SEATTLE, WASHINGTON

The Boeing Company

200,000 Square Feet

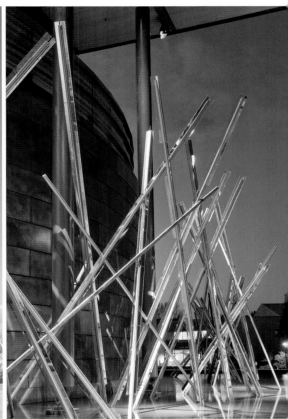

Redmond City Hall
REDMOND, WASHINGTON

City of Redmond

100,000 Square Feet

China Construction Bank

XIAMEN, CHINA

China Construction Bank

675,000 Square Feet

The Greater Tacoma
Convention and Trade Center

TACOMA, WASHINGTON

City of Tacoma

227,000 Square Feet

Jiangsu Power Company Headquarters
NANJING, CHINA

Jiangsu Provincial Power Company

753,200 Square Feet

Zhangjiang Semiconductor
Research Park - Phase 2
SHANGHAI, CHINA

ZSIP

53 Acres

Shanghai Shidong Power Company
Electric Dispatch Center
SHANGHAI, CHINA

Shidong Power Supply Co.

SMEPC

239,000 Square Feet

福州电力调度指挥中心

Fuzhou City Power
Company Headquarters
FUZHOU, CHINA

Fuzhou Electrical Power Co.

408,900 Square Feet

Microsoft - Lakeridge
REDMOND, WASHINGTON

Metzler North America

600,000 Square Feet

Zhejiang CBD Fortune
Financial Center

HANGZHOU, CHINA

Zhejiang Tefulong Real Estate

Development Ltd. Co.

1,916,000 Square Feet

SPI - Unionbay Headquarters
SEATTLE, WASHINGTON

Seattle Pacific Industries - Unionbay

94,000 Square Feet

Costco Corporate Headquarters, Building Three

ISSAQUAH, WASHINGTON

Costco Wholesale Corporation

170,000 Square Feet

Xingyue Technology Headquarters
SHANGHAI, CHINA

Xingyue Group Shanghai Investment Co., Ltd.

56 Acres

Westlake Steps

SEATTLE, WASHINGTON

Equity Office Properties

500,000 Square Feet

Huawei Beijing Environmental Technology Park Design Competition
BEIJING, CHINA

Huawei Technology Co., Ltd.

51 Acres

Competition won in November 2006

Langfang Software Park
LANGFANG, CHINA

Dalian Software Park Co. Ltd

1,615,000 Square Feet

One Twelfth @ Twelfth
BELLEVUE, WASHINGTON

Hines

480,000 Square Feet

Microsoft - Daytona
REDMOND, WASHINGTON

Hart Properties

214,000 Square Feet

Fujian Power Company Headquarters
FUZHOU, CHINA

Fujian Provincial Power

644,300 Square Feet

Stewart Street Office Building
SEATTLE, WASHINGTON

Touchstone

900,000 Square Feet

Hospitality | Residential

Seattle Grand Hyatt Hotel
SEATTLE, WASHINGTON

R.C. Hedreen

932,000 Square Feet

Dong Guan Hotel Metropolis
DONG GUAN, CHINA

South Metropolis Hotel Investment Administration Co., Ltd.

160,000 Square Feet (retail)

100,000 Square Feet (entertainment)

Lotus Resort
ABU DHABI, BAHRAIN

Apex Investment Group

90 Acres

Suifenhe Hotel and Entertainment Center

SUIFENHE, CHINA

Shimao Corporation

429,400 Square Feet

New World Center Phase II
SUZHOU, CHINA

Suzhou Sunny World Real Estate Co., Ltd.

1,200,000 Square Feet

桑拿浴
SAUNA
10.000

KTV

健身中心
FITNESS
6.000

5.000

26.900

34.100

10.000

10.000

26.900

30.500

34.100

酒店客房部
HOTEL TOWER

宴会厅
BANQUET HALL
7.000

10.000

职工宿舍
EMPLOYEE HOUSING

二期
PHASE II

酒店公寓
SERVICE
APARTMENT

Shenzhen Grand Skylight Hotel

SHENZHEN, CHINA

Shenzhen Grand Skylight Hotel Company, Ltd.

538,000 Square Feet

Seneca Street Condominiums

SEATTLE, WASHINGTON

Laconia Development, LLC

415,000 Square Feet

Escala

SEATTLE, WASHINGTON

Lexas Companies

Partnered with Thoryk Architects

820,000 Square Feet

Shanghai Fudan Crowne Plaza

SHANGHAI, CHINA

Shanghai Shangtou Investment Co. Ltd.

382,900 Square Feet

Bellevue Towers

BELLEVUE, WASHINGTON

Gerdling Edlen Development

Joint Venture with GBD Architects

1,250,000 Square Feet

Designed to LEED® Gold Standards

Retail

Costco Wholesale

WORLDWIDE

Costco Wholesale

Square Feet: Varies

Target
NATIONWIDE

Target

Square Feet: Varies

Fashion Place Mall
MURRAY, UTAH

General Growth Properties

1,277,300 Square Feet

Nike at Portland International Airport

PORTLAND, OREGON

Nike Retail Service, Inc.

1,800 Square Feet

Montclair Plaza
MONTCLAIR, CALIFORNIA

General Growth Properties

1,213,000 Square Feet

REI

NATIONWIDE

Recreational Equipment Inc.

41,600 Square Feet (average)

HANNspree

CALIFORNIA

HANNspree
Beverly Hills - 5,250 Square Feet
San Francisco - 9,500 Square Feet

Seahawks Pro Shop
SEATTLE, WASHINGTON

The Seattle Seahawks

2,900 Square Feet

Everett Riverfront

EVERETT, WASHINGTON

OliverMcMillan

Retail/Cinema/Target: 536,500 Square Feet

Hotel: 199,800 Square Feet

Westlake Shopping Center

DALY CITY, CALIFORNIA

KIMCO Realty

873,000 Square Feet

Zhengzhou East New District Walking Street

ZHENGZHOU, CHINA

Zhengzhou Xin Ao Real Estate

Development Co., Ltd.

731,900 Square Feet

Lowe's Home Improvement Warehouse

NATIONWIDE

Lowe's Companies, Inc.

170,000 Square Feet (Average)

Ashikaga Harvest Place
TOCHIGI, ASHIKAGA, JAPAN

Xymax Cube

538,200 Square Feet

Safeway

PACIFIC NORTHWEST

Safeway

Square Feet: Varies

Anthony's Restaurants
PACIFIC NORTHWEST

Anthony's Homeport, Inc.
7,000 Square Feet (average)

Xian Gaoxin
XIAN, CHINA

Xian Hi-Tech Property
Development Company
625,000 Square Feet

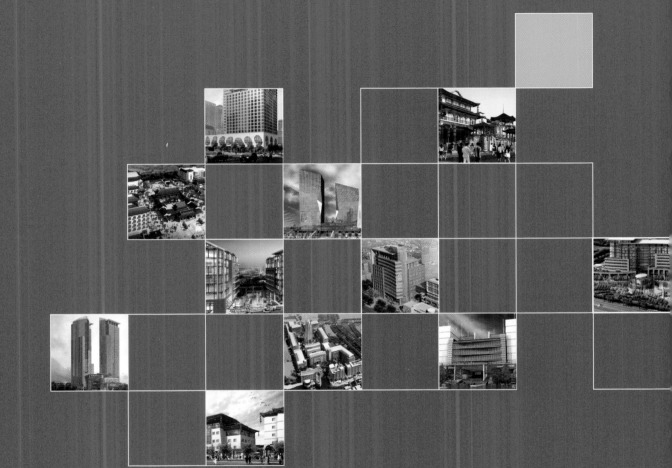

Mixed-Use

Towers on Capitol Mall

SACRAMENTO, CALIFORNIA

Saca Development

2,200,000 Square Feet

Tianmu Plaza

HANGZHOU, CHINA

Zhejiang Qianjiang Property Development Co., Ltd.

2,399,500 Square Feet

Bridge Business Park
ABU DHABI, UAE

Apex Investment Group

69 Acres

Nanjing Jingji Phase IV
NANJING, CHINA

Gold Pedestal
Real Estate Co., Ltd.
350,000 Square Feet

Xian God-Temple

XIAN, CHINA

Xian God-Temple Development Ltd. Co.

2,002,000 Square Feet

Hyatt at Olive 8
SEATTLE, WASHINGTON

R.C. Hedreen

Partnered with Gluckman Mayner Architects

650,000 Square Feet

Designed to LEED® Silver Standards

Portland City Storage
PORTLAND, OREGON

Portland City Storage

100,000 Square Feet

Designed to LEED® Gold Standards

We never forget that

people

are more important
than buildings.

There is strength in union.

Ming Zhang
SENIOR PARTNER

Mr. Zhang is the leader and visionary for MulvannyG2's designs. His creativity combined with client-centered solutions has resulted in the award of many notable projects, both domestic and international. As a leader in the design profession, his role is to lead the design, guide, teach, and influence MulvannyG2's designers to provide clients with truly inspired and relevant designs. He also oversees the firm's business development program.

Mitch Smith
SENIOR PARTNER

Mr. Smith is MulvannyG2's managing senior partner. He is responsible for providing leadership, strategic direction and management for all aspects of the firm's operations and establishing long-range business objectives. His vision and leadership has spurred record growth resulting in the firm becoming one of the top twenty largest architectural firms in the United States.

Jerry Lee
CHAIRMAN

Mr. Lee defines the attitude of the firm with his relentless practice of responding to clients' needs. His legacy has created a culture of trust and respect, charity and goodwill. Mr. Lee's dedication has been recognized by government and community leaders, and he is seated on several boards and commissions.

Balance is essential to success.

1   Corporate Headquarters
     Bellevue, Washington

2   East Coast Office
     Washington, DC

3   Southwest Office
     Irvine, California

4   Portland Office
     Portland, Oregon

5   East China Office
     Shanghai, China

6   North China Office
     Beijing, China
     (not pictured)

Photo Credits

Boeing World Headquarters
Image © Steve Keating

China Construction Bank
Image © Sheng Zhong Hai

Redmond City Hall
Image © Steve Keating

Tacoma Convention and Trade Center
Image © Steve Keating

Jiangsu Power Company Headquarters
Image © Sheng Zhong Hai

Fujian Power Company Headquarters
Image © Sheng Zhong Hai

Zhangjiang Semiconductor Research Park, Phase II
Image © Sheng Zhong Hai

Microsoft - Lakeridge
Image © Doug Scott Photography

SPI - Unionbay Headquarters
Image © Housel Photography

Costco Corporate Headquarters, Building 3
Image © Steve Keating

One Twelfth @ Twelfth
Image - Image © Doug Scott Photography

Microsoft-Daytona
Image © Steve Keating

Costco Wholesale Corporation
Image © Jeff Beck Photography
Image © David Wakely Photography

TARGET
Image © Gary Wilson

Nike at Portland International Airport
Image © Doug Scott Photography
Image © Janis Miglavs

REI
Image © Gary Wilson

HANNspree
Image © John Tenney
Image © John Sutton

Westlake Shopping Center
Image © Diane Benson
Image © Gary Silverstein

Ashikaga Harvest Place
Image © Kajima Photo Studio

QFC
Image © Robert Pisano Photography

Safeway
Image © Janis Miglavs (Bend)
Image © MulvannyG2 Architecture

Anthony's
Image © del Pozo Photography
Image © Steve Keating Photography

Lowe's
Image © Ben Benschneider

Seattle Grand Hyatt Hotel
Image © Abramowitz

Shanghai Fudan Crowne Plaza
Image © Sheng Zhong Hai

MulvannyG2 Bellevue Office Image
Image © Abramowitz
Image © Robert Pisano Photography

MulvannyG2 Washington, DC Office
Image © Joe Romeo

MulvannyG2 Irvine Office
Image © Paul Turang Photography

MulvannyG2 Portland Office
Image © Janis Miglavs